I AM
A RAINBOW

ROSEANNE D'ERASMO SCRIPT

MW01098581

This book is dedicated to my father, John Anthony D'Erasmo, who started me on my healing journey.

AuthorHouse™
1663 Liberty Drive
Bloomington, IN 47403
www.authorhouse.com
Phone: 1-800-839-8640

First published by AuthorHouse 2/21/2011

ISBN: 978-1-4567-4358-1 (sc)
Library of Congress Control Number: 2011902935

Printed in the United States of America

This book is printed on acid-free paper.

Because of the dynamic nature of the Internet, any web addresses or links contained in this book may have changed since publication and may no longer be valid. The views expressed in this work are solely those of the author and do not necessarily reflect the views of the publisher, and the publisher hereby disclaims any responsibility for them.

authorHOUSE®

References

Bailey, A. (1953) Esoteric Healing. New York: Lucis Publishing Company

Brennan, B. (1987) Hands of Light. New York: Pleiades Books

Bulbrook, M.J. (1991) Holistic Approaches to Stress Relief and Pain Management: Healing from Within and Without. Western Australia: Perth

Gerber, R. (1988) Vibrational Medicine. Santa Fe, New Mexico: Bear and Company

Judith, A. (1989) Wheels of Light. St Paul, Minneapolis: Liewlyn Publications

Mentgen, Janet & Bulbrook, M.J. (1993) Healing Touch Level 1 Notebook, Carrboro, NC: North Carolina Center for Healing Touch

Myss, C. (1996) Anatomy of the Spirit. New York: Harmony Books

www.spaceexplorers.org

On a beautiful summer evening, Joey, Marissa and their teacher walked along to the gardens of the Western land. The setting sun turned the sky a glorious red hue. Ahead of them glistened strawberries, apples, cherries, watermelons and red roses...a vision of red. Bees buzzed happily around the flowers. The teacher turned to the children and asked, "Did you know that you have a rainbow within you? Every color is there."

Marissa replied, trusting the teacher, "No, Teacher, I did not know this. How can it be? I thought I had a tummy and a back!"

"This is true, Marissa, but there is much more to your SELF. A colored rainbow is at the very center of who you are and it will be with you always."

"Hmm, sounds funny to me," said Joey. "Tell me more, please."

"There are seven main places of energy in your body and each one has its own color. Let's talk about your centers, starting with the root. It is at the base of your spine, the lower part of your body. You will feel it tingle as you remain still, and think about being alive, strong and grounded."

"Safe, too?" asked Marissa.

"Yes, dear one, feeling safe is a connection with the root, the first energy center, with its color red. Look around at the garden and see the colors of red so you can think of red any time at all. Listen to the drums and the buzzing of the bees, for these are the sounds of the first energy center."

So Marissa and Joey looked at all the red colors of the flowers and fruits and soaked in the beautiful crimson sunset that surrounded them.

"We are walking the earth with a feeling that everything is connected," explained the teacher.

"I think I understand. At least I can see the color red all around and I feel pretty happy!" exclaimed Joey. "I'm making a picture in my head."

"Yes Joey, that is your mind's eye," explained Teacher.

As Marissa and Joey walked along with their teacher, they came upon a stream, covered by a bridge, which overlooked a garden of pumpkins, orange tiger lilies, bundles of orange leaves and bushels of oranges. The sunset had turned orange as it often does over time. The children twirled in delight as they crossed the bridge and bathed in the splendid color of orange. In the distance was the lovely sound of a flute, the sound of the next energy point.

"Wow, I guess we've come to orange!" cried Marissa.

"Yes, that's right! Orange is the color of the area right below your belly button. It is called your sacral. Just put your hands there and think of the color orange."

"This may sound strange," said Joey, "but my eyes are watery and I am tingling around my belly button all the way through to my back."

"Me too," whispered Marissa.

"Very good, children. That is what it feels like to bring energy to an area. You will feel creative, having new thoughts and ideas as you think of the color orange."

"Yippee!" they exclaimed in delight.

The children looked up and suddenly, it was as if a new day was beginning, with a different color in the Eastern land beyond. Marissa thought this must be a dream, but it felt so real…the teacher, the land, the colors and the bright yellow sun. Maybe they should just keep walking to see what all this was really about. They followed the faint sound of violins.

"Teacher, look at the yellow lemons and the little yellow canary," said Joey.

"I see a field of buttercups and big bunches of ripe yellow bananas," cried Marissa. "And look at the pretty bushes of little yellow flowers."

"Those are forsythias, children. We are surrounded by yellow, the color of your third energy point, the solar plexus. It is about two inches above your belly button. You may feel it tingle as you laugh, or when you are angry."

"Teacher, I am feeling like I am part of a great big family," said Marissa.

"Yes, sweet child, that is the family of man. Soak in the beauty of the yellow rays of the sun and the garden of daffodils."

"I am feeling like I want to help somebody," said Joey.

"Good, Joey, you are making the connection. See the circle of fire over there? Fire and a circle are symbols of this energy point. Know that the solar plexus is the source of ambition, courage and generosity. Feel great strength and intelligence. All this comes from your third energy point, my children."

"I feel buzzing from my toes to my tummy," hummed Marissa.

The teacher noticed that Joey and Marissa had three small circles of red, orange and yellow spinning to the right at each energy point and could see that the children were learning. The teacher was pleased.

So the teacher and children continued on their journey and traveled over the bridge at the end of the yellow garden, coming upon rolling hills of luscious green grass. Moss-covered trees created a canopy over a garden of green plants. In the center of the hills was a valley with a green pond with frogs jumping from lily pad to lily pad! They could hear bells ringing in the distance.

"Oh, I see green all around, Teacher. I feel light as a feather!" exclaimed Joey.

"Your fourth energy point, the heart, is the focus for love, radiance and wisdom," explained the teacher. "You will feel a powerful sense of love within this center. Its color is green."

"Would that be like a feeling of love for *everybody*?" asked Marissa.

"Yes, my child."

"Teacher, I like this feeling," said Joey. "I feel A-Okay!"

"You will feel lovable and capable and good about yourself. Children, this is the center of healing, trust, hope and dreams. You may use this energy as a healer."

"You mean we can learn to heal?" questioned Marissa.

"Oh yes, that will come in time. You can let go and release all your troubles to a Divine plan."

"Just let it go, Teacher?" inquired Joey.

"Letting go, that is the language of forgiveness; to know that no one has control over love in your life."

"Hmm...I feel peaceful," said Joey.

"Yes, you will reach a state of tranquility that helps you feel inner peace," explained Teacher.

And so the teacher and children lay upon the grass, feeling all that Mother Earth has to offer, basking in the surrounding shades of green.

As they stood to continue their journey, they came upon a crystal blue lake framed by a deep blue sky. They heard the chirping of bluebirds and were welcomed by fields of bluebells and blueberries.

"Here comes blue!" remarked Joey. "Oh, Marissa's blue eyes are shining at me."

"You are so smart, dear one. Blue is the color of your throat, your fifth center. When this center is well and whole, you will feel peaceful, calm and creative and you will communicate well with those around you."

"Teacher, I hear the wind through the trees as I close my eyes," said Marissa.

"Very good, child. This is the sound connected with the fifth center. Your true nature or purpose in life is shown to you at this point. It is the sense of yourself within, a place where you will have a clear vision of your choices."

"Teacher, I *do* feel that I have choices and that I should believe in myself," said Joey.

"That's exactly right. Your ability to keep your word is a strength of the fifth center and you will feel more in touch with your own inner truth as you bring energy to your throat. All illness has a connection here because choice is involved in every detail of our lives."

"Oh Teacher, I can see how important choosing is. But sometimes, there are too many choices!" said Marissa.

"Yes! For this throat center is the center of both choice and consequence. The key to the fifth center is faith. Faith and power of choice are the power of creation itself. We are asked to make choices that unite the mind and heart."

"I think, Teacher, that this is very good advice, but it must be difficult to bring together the mind and the heart," said Joey very thoughtfully.

"Some say that it is the longest journey one has to travel, from the mind to the heart. You learn so quickly, my children."

They remained under the blue sky for a while, soaking in the many shades of blue. The children felt sleepy and so they dozed. Upon awakening, they noticed it was a bit darker. The sky had turned to a color that was in-between purple and blue. It reminded them of the color of ink pens. They heard rushing water, as though a waterfall was nearby.

"Teacher, what has happened?" asked Marissa. "It is getting dark. Have we been asleep for a long time?"

"Children, you are safe. The sky has turned dark to teach us about indigo, the color of our sixth energy point, your brow. If you mix deep blue with purple, you will see the color indigo."

"I see that, Teacher, all around me," yawned Joey.

"Your sixth center is located between your eyebrows. It is sometimes called your third eye. It is the seat of your mind. Intuition, compassion and wisdom are here. You may see a six-pointed star as you bring energy to this center. You will have great dreams and a bright imagination as this center becomes active."

"I am seeing the night sky and the stars and I am thinking about the tomorrows of my life," shared Marissa.

"Yes, dear child. You will create real visions of your future as you begin to feel one with the universe. You will realize that ideas come before creation and it all begins with energy. When you are not afraid, you can see the truth. You will be wise and see clearly."

"I feel myself opening up, like a flower," said Marissa.

"Yes, you may see the lotus flower in your mind, a symbol of this point."

The sky became lighter, the color of violet, as they continued their walk. Ahead, lilac trees graced their path. The flower garden was filled with purple violets, pansies and delphiniums.

"Teacher, we must be at the end of the rainbow, I am finally understanding," said Joey. "We started with red and now we have arrived at purple!"

"Yes, you are right. Let us move our thoughts to our seventh center, the crown, which is governed by the color violet. This energy point is often called the seat of the soul. It is located at the top of your head. It is the center of your higher will, thought and information. You will feel a sense of happiness as this center becomes active. This is where you connect with spirit, a higher power or universal good. It is the point of prayer."

"So, we might see purple in our mind as we pray?" asked Joey.

"Well, that is possible. What you may want to do is actually bring the color purple to mind as you pray, instead of waiting for it," explained Teacher.

"I love purple," said Marissa. "I feel so peaceful in a purple room. But Teacher, how do we hold on to these lovely feelings?"

"My children, the lesson is to live in the moment," said the teacher. "Let us review your knowledge. You have seven main energy points that are in charge of life, communication, love, learning, health, illness and dreams. You can give energy to your centers by thinking of their colors and places in your body."

"But Teacher, how do we remember all that we have learned and still bring energy to our centers?" asked Joey.

"Meditation will help you. But learning how to meditate is for another day when we will explore the aspects of going within."

"Okay, Teacher," said Marissa.

The teacher turned to the children and said, "We can see rainbows after rain showers. We can see rainbows from outer space. We can see rainbows inside ourselves. The rainbow of life is the essence of who we are. It is the substance of our life on Earth. We are:

Rainbows of the World,

Rainbows of Life,

Rainbows of Self."

"I can feel and can see that *I Am a Rainbow*!" said Joey.

"And I Am a Rainbow!" echoed Marissa.

The teacher and children walked home together all warm and tingly. And if you look ever so closely you can see their rainbows glowing as they walk.

CPSIA information can be obtained
at www.ICGtesting.com
Printed in the USA
LVIC081222160413
329361LV00001B

9 781456 743581